A

LETTER

TO

GEORGE STEEVENS, ESQ.

AMS PRESS
NEW YORK

A

LETTER

TO

GEORGE STEEVENS, ESQ.

CONTAINING

A CRITICAL EXAMINATION

OF THE

PAPERS OF SHAKSPEARE;

PUBLISHED BY

MR. SAMUEL IRELAND.

TO WHICH ARE ADDED,

EXTRACTS FROM VORTIGERN.

BY JAMES BOADEN, ESQ.
AUTHOR OF FONTAINVILLE FOREST, &c.

Perfectos veteresque referri debet, an inter
Viles atque novos?

HORACE.

LONDON:

PRINTED FOR MARTIN AND BAIN, FLEET-STREET,

MDCCXCVI.

Library of Congress Cataloging in Publication Data

Boaden, James, 1762-1839.
  A letter to George Steevens, esq.

  1. Ireland, William Henry, 1777-1835. Miscellaneous
papers and legal instruments under the hand and seal
of William Shakespeare. 2. Shakespeare, William,
1564-1616--Forgeries--Ireland. I. Steevens, George,
1736-1800. II. Title.
PR2950.A23B6 1972   822.3'3   74-39459
ISBN 0-404-00916-6

Reprinted from the edition of 1796, London
First AMS edition published in 1972
Manufactured in the United States of America

International Standard Book Number: 0-404-00916-6

AMS PRESS INC.
NEW YORK, N. Y.   10003

TO

GEORGE STEEVENS, Esq.

DEAR SIR,

UPON a subject so deeply interesting as Shakspeare, I believe no apology will be necessary for offering to your perusal the following pages. Your laborious researches enable you, in a very superior degree, to confirm the remarks they contain, or establish the authenticity of what it is their avowed purpose to examine.

When a report first went abroad, that Mr. Ireland, of Norfolk Street, had made a discovery so important as the papers of Shakspeare, the writer of these sheets went to see them, and was very politely allowed by their possessor to hear him read them at leisure. In some instances credulity is no disgrace:—strong enthusiasm is always eager to believe. I confess, therefore,

that

that, for some time after I had seen them, I continued to think they might be genuine. They bore the character of the poet's writing—the paper appeared of sufficient age—the water-marks were earnestly displayed, and the matter diligently applauded.——To a mind filled with the most ardent love and the most eager zeal, disarmed of caution by the character too of the gentleman who displayed them, it will not be a subject of severe reproof, that the wished impression was made. I remember, that I beheld the papers with the tremor of the purest delight—touched the invaluable relics with reverential respect, and deemed even existence dearer, as it gave me so refined a satisfaction. He, who has long combatted with the arts of literary imposture, may smile at the simplicity of this avowal, although he should be unable to refuse his praise to the candour by which it has been dictated.

In what manner distrust first entered my mind, I think it unnecessary to state, farther than that my doubts were accumulated from the reflection in my closet upon circumstances recorded; examining those facts scrupulously by the light of history; and applying to things the rule of chronology, and to persons the records of biography. I found myself speedily entangled in perplexities, and at war with known events.—In few words,

all

all of the knowledge I had received as undeniable, all of the fact I had relied on as true, was of necessity to be sacrificed to the new creed of the recent discoveries. I went no more—and blushed that, innocently, for a short time, I had, in the small circle of my friends, allowed myself to aid the cause of deception. The book is at length before the public; and the very gentleman, who published it, I trust will have no reason to complain of the *manner* in which I pursue my examinations.

The writer is willing to meet Mr. IRELAND in the way he desires to be met.—There are persons who say, " give us up the name of the gentle-
" man, at whose house they were found, and
" we will believe."—An assertion that seems to throw down the science of criticism under the testimony of character. It is of no importance at all NOW from whom they came to Mr. Ireland—this knowledge at first might have had some effect in *legal* consideration—but, if I am to accept these papers upon credit, I would take the belief of Mr. Ireland himself as readily as that of any gentleman of whatever *property*—unless indeed it could be shewn, that science and wealth were concomitants; and that he, who was " spa-
" cious in the possession of dirt," must naturally have the most enlarged understanding, and the

most

[4]

most vigorous and penetrating sagacity. What is not therefore convenient for Mr. Ireland to state, I have not the slightest desire to know.— By *internal* evidence alone these papers must be judged; and if, that shall be found irrefragable, it is of no moment where they have been buried, or by what nefarious process they may have been for years secreted from the public eye, and withheld from the lineal inheritor.

Undoubtedly this subject will be examined by skill infinitely beyond that, which this writer possesses; greater than he has even faculties to attain.—But Truth will collect all the scattered rays of criticism, and those, which separately have little light or heat, by her power of concentration, may carry irresistible force—

" Thoughts that breathe and words that *burn.*"

Mr. Ireland confesses, that some account may properly be expected of the manner in which these papers came into his hands—" He received
" them, he therefore readily adds, ftom his son
" *Samuel William Henry Ireland, a
" young

* Such a man as Mr. Malone would naturally wish to examine the register of this youth's baptism—but I sincerely believe that, by the power of *prophetic illumination*, he was
called

[5]

" young man then under 19 years of age; by
" whom the discovery was accidentally made at
" the house of a gentleman of considerable pro-
" perty." I believe this young gentleman is
under a Solicitor, applying to the study of the
law; and mention the circumstance, *solely*, to
prove how naturally he might be led to search
among forgotten deeds, and mouldy parchments,
and to carry to his father with eagerness the first
fruits of his research. Upon any expressions
of this youth, which friendship may not have
guarded with becoming confidence, it is not my
wish to expatiate—neither shall I notice the name
of TALBOT for any other purpose, than to state
his assertion, that they were found in *his* company, and that this person, an actor,

Is HE, whom mutual *league*,
United *thoughts*, and *counsels*, equal *hope*
And *hazard* in the GLORIOUS ENTERPRIZE,
Join'd with him ONCE.

Of the honour claimed by the publication, it
was thought necessary to give him his full share—
the writer understood, that, in Ireland, he declared
his resolution to claim it;—and, with the best
wishes for his success, he now proceeds to the

called WILLIAM HENRY after his ancestor, who, TWO CEN-
TURIES *before his birth*, saved the life of his friend SHAKS-
PEARE!!

examination

examination of the structure from which that honour must be derived.

I observe that, in the preface to the volume, Mr. Ireland, with the speed that is natural to good taste, hurries over the instruments of legal acts, to come to the copy of LEAR, which he has given us entire. And upon this subject his remark is at once curious and useful.

" To the man of *taste*, and lover of *simplicity*, to the *sound* CRITIC, it is conceived, upon collating them, it will appear, that the alterations made in the *printed* copies of LEAR are manifestly introduced by the *players*, and are deviations from that *spontaneous flow of soul* and *simple diction*, which so eminently distinguish this great **author of nature*; and that the *additions* and *alterations* interspersed, which, in the eyes of the players, were no doubt splendid improvements, have not unfrequently been introduced at the expence of the natural course of the narrative, the regular detail of

---

* This idolatrous folly will shew the competent knowledge of the writer in language.

" Stripping JOVE's statue of his oaken wreath,
" To hang up to the memory of a man."

COWPER.

" the

" the fact, and the uniformity of the author's
" style; which, whether it is employed on great
" things or small, in expressing humble or lofty
" images is *invariably without labour or effort,*
" and without any thing like *hardness or inver-*
" *sion:* These too are amongst the reasons, that
" have persuaded the editor, that these papers
" are genuine; for, it is presumed, the MS.
" here presented to the public must have been
" the original, and probably the *only one* by the
" author."

When I read this passage first, I own it filled me with astonishment—I could scarcely believe the evidence of the sense, that presented criticism so despicably shallow, and assertion so miserably fallacious. It at once converted the PLAYERS into the most elaborate and polished masters of versification, and SHAKSPEARE into a writer without the necessary ear for rhythm— a man who produced a series of harmonious versification by chance, and lost the supreme ascendancy in his art, from the not being able to number ten syllables upon his fingers. In the following remarks upon this pretended unsophisticated LEAR, I shall fully discuss this point among others.

It is probable that, in the whole compass of English versification, the critic can find no writer of verse modulated with greater skill than the lines of Shakspeare. He fills the ear as much as the mind, and employs the utmost extent of sonorous and majestic eloquence. In his efforts after the lofty and the sublime, he is frequently turgid and diffuse; his meaning is often buried under the pomp of his expression, and a very feeble thought lies like a titled idiot entombed in marble, and surrounded by the graces of too lavish art. Such is the defect of him, who, if he had not thus erred, would have been too perfect for humanity. As the most satisfactory evidence of this great truth, we may refer with confidence to the book of Bishop HURD, who had accumulated, according to the idea of Dr. JOHNSON, all his innovations upon language as monuments to his honour. With Shakspeare came more compound epithets than all our previous writers had displayed; and those in an art which, more than any other, might have been contented with simplicity of phrase, as it had more in its province than other branches of literature, the representation of human passions by the aid of character and action. In descriptive or didactic poetry, language may frequently be found unequal to the conveyance of an impression, adequate to the

liveliness

liveliness of the object we describe, or the power of the precept we would inculcate. But the drama is the reflection of life and passion, of character and manners, and these express themselves in the simplest language, unless the poet, decorating as well as delineating, bestow the colours of his art upon the figure he exhibits. So nice and curious is this art, that something is derived from the collocation of sounds, independent both of justness in the sense and metrical exactness in the numbers.—The sense without this garb is not poetry, be it ever so pregnant; and though the syllables should scan with the utmost correctness, the requisite number would never constitute poetry, unless they had the glowing diction, which results from the happiest choice of words in the sweetest consonancy of numbers, combining with the ideas of the poet, selected from character, and vivified by genius.

How fondly have the whole race of critics and readers been attributing this exalted excellence to the muse of Shakspeare! and how weakly have they pardoned redundancy and inflation in some instances, for the prevailing grandeur characteristic of his lines. If we are to believe this new critic, his verse habitually ran into all the laxity of prose; whether upon a lofty or an humble image, he expresses himself at all times without *labour* or *effort*; and all the *hardness* and *inversion* we meet with were foisted into his works by his own PLAYERS, and considered by them to be *beauties*—nay, where they gave the flow of metre to a rumbling line of 15 syllables, and added vigour to the sentiment, while they compressed its language, SHAKSPEARE, the loose and easy Shakspeare, abjured the amendments, and doomed us, by will, to read only the bald dissonance locked up in his old cedar chest.

But the present is not an age in which this wretched ignorance can find credit.—The labours of such men as Dr. JOHNSON, Dr. Farmer, Mr. Tyrwhitt, Mr. Malone, (and allow me, Sir, to add the name of STEEVENS to the list) have not been thrown away so entirely, as not to have led us to juster conclusions, and to more rational principles of decision. We know, that the greatest faults are on the confines of the greatest beauties—that men partake the general fashion of their times in *literature* and in *dress*; that, at the revival of letters, it was natural even for SHAKSPEARE to be *tumid*; and we see, in degree, this mark of the period he lived in impressed upon all his writings. Let not any blemishes of this kind be deemed to derogate from the fame of the poet—with the true critic they will augment his reputation—they are only the cloudy encrustations of a gem, intrinsically beyond all
comparison

comparison for lustre and magnitude. While we lament the grosser impurities of an age, severe in moral and relaxed in habit, let us survey with regret any occasional efforts to gild the wings of fancy with unnecessary splendor.

But such a critic as the person whose words I quote, may be apt to exclaim " Treason against " the *spontaneous flow of the soul* of the sweet " Swan of AVON!—Would you deny this *honied-* " *tongued* AUTHOR OF NATURE the character of " *simplicity?*" What is said particularly is not a general position; and, although I think his logic nearly as despicable as his taste, I will yet trust him with my sentiments upon the simplicity of Shakspeare; and rely upon better discernment than his, to prevent its perversion.

Undoubtedly the works of Shakspeare contain abundant instances of the sweetest simplicity of thought; and many independent speeches may be selected written with the gentlest suavity of numbers and diction; but simplicity is not the character of his serious muse, and his pathos is constantly intermitted by some laboured subtlety of conceit or some magnificent diffusion of sentiment. To say that his muse is never *hard* nor *inverted*, never *laboured* nor *affected*, would be to leave indeed the skeleton of his dialogue in all his tragedies and historical dramas. His plenitude of expression always operates as a snare to him—his mine of language is inexhaustible, and his persistency of toil produces more wealth than the occasion demands.—His idea like his own HAL

"Seeks for the greatness that will overwhelm it."

To change the metaphor, when he has drank of the river, he delights his ear with the roaring of its fall—he lingers at the source of his delight, and quits its gratifications slowly and with reluctance. I am compelled to say that the criticism which called forth the observation is the only sort by which the publication can be justified; and when we are seriously requested to believe, that, writing English verse, the poet made Edgar say

"And with ADAM-like nakedness out-face
"The winde and persecution of the sky."

instead of

"And with *presented* nakedness," &c.

and that the players not feeling the "*spontaneous flow of a soul.*" which could thus emit the most untuneable quaintness, without the "slightest degree of *hardness*," supposed they were improving it (rugged souls!) by the interpolation of the word *presented,* when such things are seriously affirmed, happy is the pseudo Shakspeare in his
Critic,

Critic, and the critic in his bard; superior is the commentator to the contempt he provokes, and the poet must be narrowly searched in the behalf of SHAKSPEARE.

> " He does here usurp
> " The name he owes not; and has put himself
> " Upon this island, as a thief to win it
> " From him the lord on't."—
>
> TEMPEST.

But it may be said by those who receive the *quantity* as evidence, or at any rate, presumption of the authenticity of the LEAR, how are you enabled so peremptorily to pronounce it spurious? much of it necessarily is found in the printed books; are the passages which differ in themselves sufficiently decisive of the question?—I answer I think that they are, and I hope shall be able to convince any reader that they are, from an examination of the various editions published in the life-time of the poet, and after his decease. And this examination naturally divides itself into three heads of consideration, passages altered and passages omitted or altogether newly introduced, of all which in their order. But previously to the discussion, is there nothing let me ask upon the surface, at which the intelligent reader starts? How is the page in its general complexion, in what condition does its *orthography* appear? Is it after any received system, is it uniformly particular,

cular, or does it set at defiance the spelling of all periods, and bring to the recollection the only typographic parallel in the forgeries of Chatterton? Look at the authors from whose orthography the poet must have derived his knowledge of language, and from whose pages we can form alone any guess of the orthography of his times, how decide they? Look at Hollinshead and the poets from whose records and tales he has drawn the materials of his dramas, is there in all or one of these or any other writers, a single example of language so idle in its literal form, so clogged, so confounded by unnecessary letters? Be not alarmed, gentle reader, that I am about to enter into any tedious disquisition upon the subject; but we know well how the liberal use of the letters *y* and *e* tend to the giving a semblance of antiquity; and when that prodigious youth CHATTERTON composed his surprising poems we find him unsparing in the use also of *nne*; but his most sanguine efforts after these "ancient incumbrances" never reached the exhibition of such words as innetennecyonne, innevennecyonne and others of similar composition. SPENCER is an author, for his time even, unusually lax in orthography, and the difficulties of his stanza compelled him to frequent innovations, to produce what, to the eye at least, should look like the termination of rhymes. He preceded the poet and remark his orthography.

An

An instance or two are given without selection as they occur upon opening his volume.

> " So well hee woo'd her, and so well he wrought her,
> " With faire entreety and fweet blandishment
> " That at the length, unto a bay he brought her,
> " So as shee to his speeches was content
> " To lend an ear and softly to relent."

Let it not be forgotten that some of the plays of Shakspeare were printed while he was in the zenith of his reputation, and it is believed from his own copies. At least the copies of the theatre of which he was a proprietor. Mr. IRELAND asserts him to have been in the habit of bargaining with booksellers for his pieces, to him therefore the argument is valid—How do they appear? Is there in the ROMEO and JULIET, for instance, printed by JOHN DANTER, in 1597, before it was augmented by the author, any orthography like that of Mr. Ireland's MSS. I select,

> " Vertue itselfe turns vice being misapplied,
> " And vice sometimes by action dignified.
> " Within the infant rinde of this small flower
> " Poyson hath residence and medicine power."

Quarto, 1597.

What is the spelling of that very play of LEAR published in his life-time also, 1608, will be seen when I come to confront the copies, and to demand why passages, upon which Shakspeare has obviously set his seal, are omitted in the edition of Mr. Ireland?

Ireland? For that they are *his*, and not interpolations by the players, shall be obvious to any man competent to decide upon the evidence of thought and diction, notwithstanding the editor's probability that this is the only copy that came from the hands of the poet. Yet upon what does this most sagacious critic infer that it is so? Is it upon the ground of its gross impurities by which the meaning of many passages is destroyed? Is it because it follows invariably the worst reading where the readings are various? Is it because it cuts the knot of difficulties, which a legitimate copy would naturally untie? or is it because a whole scene is omitted in which a passage occurs that baffles all *conjectural emendation? These assertions I do not desire to be received as probabilities, from their being asserted; I will prove all of them in the most satisfactory manner, and establish that it is an unskilfully executed and manifest delusion.

---

* I mean that which stands the 3d scene in the 4th act, and to be found only in the quarto. The difficulty I allude to is in the passage, where the Queen's behaviour is described upon the knowledge of her father's savage treatment by her sisters.

" You have seen
" Sunshine and rain at once: her smiles and tears
" Were a like a *better way*."

This has eluded the grasp of our master critics, and, therefore

" Shall dunghill curs confront the helicons?"

It

It is here very likely I shall be asked, what I think of the various *other* papers discovered, and of the books in which the remarks of Shakspeare are to be found in his own hand-writing? —My answer shall be a very short story, equally pithy and profitable, and " righte pleasaunte untoe antiquariaunes."

A collector of scarce books once called upon a bookseller, and told him, that he had lately bought at his shop, a very rare volume, which he found by certain signs in the margin, had belonged to Oliver Cromwell, the Protector. The bookseller desired to see the evidence alluded to, and was shewn the letters *O. C. P.* denoting, in the judgment of the buyer, Oliver Cromwell, *Protector*. The tradesman, with much coolness, remarked, that his only astonishment was, how the *O* should come there? for, as to the *C* and the *P* he wrote them himself upon the book, to signify that it was—*collated* and found *perfect*.

COLLATIONS AND REMARKS.

The first circumstance I think it necessary to remark is, that diligent collation of the printed copies with the Lear just published, has enabled me me to decide, that the writer of the manuscript at first used only the 2d folio edition, with such modern impressions, as he might chance to possess—although, in the course of the play, he acquires evidently a copy of BUTTER's QUARTO, 1608, and uses it with so determined a preference over the folio, that he preserves its readings to the absolute injury of the sense of the passages. The folio 1623 he does not appear to have seen. The first proof which is offered, occurs in the bequest of Lear to Gonerill. The words, which we find in the folio—

> " and with champaines rich'd
> " With plenteous rivers"—

are in Mr. Ireland's edition, and are not in the quarto.

The second instance is in the following scene, where by mistake *Cordelia* is made to announce the approach of France and Burgundy in the folio instead of *Gloucester*, who had been sent to conduct them into the presence. The quarto corrects this; but by the writer of Mr. Ireland's play, this book had not been then seen. SHAKSPEARE himself could never so grossly err as to exhibit the modest, the silent Cordelia, foremost to announce the entrance of her own suitors.

But

[19]

But when the transcriber of this play had seen the quarto, it is curious to remark the glaring absurdity into which blind and undiscerning confidence plunges him at whatever hazard. The execration which LEAR utters against the ungrateful and savage Gonerill, is thus given in the 2d folio.

" Heare Nature, heare, deare Goddesse, heare:
" Suspend thy purpose, if thou didst intend
" To make this creature fruitfull:
" Into her wombe convey sterility,
" Dry up in her the organs of increase,
" And from her derogate body, never spring
" A Babe to honor her. If she must teeme
" Create her child of spleene, that it may live
" And be a thwart disnatur'd to her.
" Let it stampe wrinkles in her brow of youth,
" With cadent Teares fret channels in her cheekes,
" Turne all her mother's paines and benefits
" To laughter, and contempt: That she may feele,
" How sharper than a serpent's tooth it is
" To have a thankelesse childe. Away, away."

I blush to present the reader with the *nonsensical*, disjointed, inconclusive and mutilated form, in which, upon the authority of Mr. Ireland's MSS. we are to receive this from the hand of SHAKSPEARE.—It is faithfully copied.

" Itte maye bee soe *harke* Nature heare deare Goddesse
" Suspende thy purpose iffe thou wouldst make thys
" Creature fruitefull Intoe herre wombe conveye
" Sterylytye drye uppe inne herre the organnes offe

" Innecrease

> " Innecrease ande lette noe babe sprynge toe honorre herre
> " butte iffe she muste teeme create herre childe of spleene
> " and lette itte channelle rynkles onne herre browe
> " of Youthe with *accente* teares turne alle herre paynes
> " toe rude laughterree and contempte Thatte she maye
> " knowe howe sharpe ande lyke a serpente's toothe it is
> " toe have a thanklesse childe."

accente teares are to be found in the quarto. Before this occurs a speech of Edmund's in the quarto of some length which he has not taken. A *curse* seems to be fatal to the writer of the MS. as the following will further establish.

> " thatte these hotte teares thatte breake fromme
> " mee perforce shoud make worse blasts ande Foggs
> " onne the unnetennederre woundynges of a Fatherres
> " usse playe thys parte agayne &c."

As it is impossible that either Shakspeare should write this, or any human being comprehend it, if he did, the passage is added from the folio, 1632.

> " That these hot teares, which breake from me perforce
> " Should *make thee worth them.*
> " Blasts and Fogges upon thee :
> " Th' untented woundings of a Father's curse
> " *Pierce every sense about thee. Old fond eyes*
> " *Beweepe thee* once againe I'le plucke ye out
> " And cast you with the waters that you loose
> " To temper clay."

There is an absolute necessity for the words printed above in Italics, to afford the sufficient chain

chain of language and the progress as well as nature of the thoughts. That the reader of these extracts may not be embarrassed with needless difficulties, arising from the mere appearance of these passages from the MS. of Shakspeare, the following orthographical instances are here presented him.

Innefyrmytyes	Infirmities
Unnefreynnedidde	Unfriended
adoppetedde	adopted
dyshonnorredde	dishonoured
unnepryzedde	unpriz'd
Burregannedye	Burgundy
scannetedde	scanted
slennederrelye	slenderly
dymennesyonnes	dimensions
perrepennedycularelye	perpendicularly
* helas	alas

When these are become familiar to the eye, the only difficulty will be to attain the sense of the passages I now proceed to select—hoping that the " spontaneous flow of the soul of our bard" may carry conviction to every heart, and enable us to discard all the manifest interpolations by which the players imagined they restored to common

* By this curious mode of writing the interjection, one might be tempted to believe that Shakspeare had received a French education at the College of St. Omers.

sense,

sense, passages, which to their limited understandings, afforded no distinct meaning.

I find in the MS.

> " Kill thy physician and thy fee bestow
> " Upon the *Soule* disease."

This I conjecture happened from the *f* in the folio not being plainly crossed, and the writers wanting the perception of the nonsense he was producing by making it an *S*.

When EDMUND comments upon the excellent foppery of the world, and observes that

> " We make guilty of our disasters *the sun*,
> " *The moon, the stars,* as if we were villains
> " On necessity."

In the MS. disasters are not followed by any consequences, and the verb is left without any subject to which it can be referred, for thus it is given by Mr. Ireland.

" Wee make guiltye of oure dysasterres
" Vyllaynes bye niscessytye fooles bye compulsyonne," &c.

In the droggrel rhymes uttered by the foole instead of *whore*, which however coarse is essential to the rhyme, we find the word *hope* and verse is printed as prose. SHAKSPEARE not knowing the forms of metrical arrangement.

" Leave

" Leave thy drinke and thy *hope* [whore]
" And keep in a door,
" And thou shalt have more
" Than two tens to a score."

From whatever cause the extravagancies of this *worthy* fool, are singularly given in the hand writing of Shakspeare. The words in Italics are omitted in the MS. and the whole printed as prose.

" Then they for joy did weep,
" And I for sorrow sung
" That such a king should play bopeep,
" *And go the fools among.*"

In the passage a little before we have

" Truth's a dog must to kennel while my lady [o'th' brache or broache]
" May stand by the fire and stink."

The words in hooks are omitted, and I take an opportunity of starting a conjecture that we should read for Lady Brach, *Lady o'th Broach* [Turnspit]

" *Foole.*
" The hedge sparrow fed the cuckow so long
" That it had its head bit off by its younge."

The quarto and Mr. Ireland's MS. read

" Thatte itte hadde the heade be itte younge."

Lear's train in the MS. is made to consist of

" *Four* hundreth knyghtes and squires"

although

although the number *one* hundred is sufficiently marked in the course of the play.

The following passage is an additional proof of the clearness of this, which is called the original copy of the play—The common reading is

" Such smiling rogues
" Like rats, oft bite the holy cords in twain
" Which are too intrinse t' unloose: smooth every passion
" That in the natures of their lords rebels."

which our miraculous MS. displays in the following unclouded light.

" Like ratts nibble those cordes inne twaine,
" Which are toe intrenche ande loosen everye smooth passyon."

For with *presented* nakedness, &c. we are favoured with the following

" And with *A-dam-like* nakedness outface
" The wynde ande persecutione of the skye."

If this be meant for metre, it is dissonance! if it be given as an improved reading, it is folly. When Adam was naked, the elements were yet unagitated; and when creation was punished for his transgression, Adam was no longer naked.

EDGAR, a few lines below, purposes to conceal himself, and he therefore adds to the squalid habit of the madman and beggar, the prayers, the lunatic banns, and ejaculations of the characters.

" Poor

[25]

> " Poor Turlygood, poor Tom!
> " That's something yet—Edgar I nothing am."

This it is to have players for the editors of an author's works. Shakspeare, says Mr. Ireland, gave it,

> " Poore Tom, poore Edgarre.
> " Thatte innedeede is somethynge. I amme nothynge."

Meaning thus most sagaciously to use that name in his exclamations, which must alarm the suspicions of any, who might be commissioned to seek him; and who, knowing, that from any port it was impossible he should escape, would be confident that in disguize he lurked in some part of the kingdom.

When the reader has read the following awful address, he will hardly away with what must follow it (not Heaven knows for preferment).

> " Let the great gods
> " That keep this dreadful pudder o'er our heads,
> " Find out their enemies now. Tremble thou wretch,
> " That hast within thee undivulged crimes,
> " Unwhipped of justice: Hide thee, thou bloody hand;
> " Thou perjur'd, and thou simular of virtue
> " That art incestuous: Caitiff, to pieces shake,
> " That under covert and convenient seeming
> " Has practis'd on man's life! Close pent-up guilts,
> " Rive your concealing continents, and cry
> " These dreadful summoners grace. I am a man
> " More sinn'd against than sinning."

[Folio 1632.]

From Mr. Ireland's Lear.

" Lette the greate Gods, who thunderre oere oure heades
" Fynde theyre Enemyes nowe tremble thou wretche
" Thatte haste withinne thee undyvulgedde Crymes
" Hyde thee thou bloudye hande unwhypte of Justice
" Thou Sycophante dissemblerre of Virtewe
" Ande convenyente seemynge thatte practysedde
" Close pente uppe guiltes onne credulouse Mens lives
" Rive youre concealedde Centerres ande begge grace
" Offe these Greate ande thunderynge Summonerres
" Butte I amme oune more synnd agaynste thenne synnyng"

For the comprehensive precept of Edgar

" Keep thy word justly; swear not; commit not with man's sworne spouse;"

The book of SHAKSPEARE, the only one that ever came from his hand; every line of which he had numbered to prevent the slightest augmentation or decrease, reads the following sound morality:

" Keepe thye worde ande whore with man's sworne spouse."

But enough and more than enough of such palpable proof.

" Never count the turns—One and a million!"

This has in plain truth been the most irksome part of my task. with the readings of the best copies in my remembrance to read the new publication was a source of astonishment and laughter. To extract the passages with fidelity has been an employment of difficulty and disgust,

de-

deformed as they are by almost impossible errors, and a vicious and fantastic orthography, with not a point (there is not even so much as a period) to conduct the disunited members of sentences to any junction; with verse perpetually distended into prose by the intrusion of expletives and the disarrangement of words; and every species of perversion which the most determined enemy to sense and poetry could have the ingenuity to inflict.

Let us hear no more of the carelessness of HEMINGE and CONDELL!—They were compared with the poet himself, the correctest writers, the most judicious critics, the most elegant of poets. For one absurdity in their copy he has left an hundred in his MSS. and if we regard versification as a merit, it must be severed from this spontaneous writer.—His Lear contains no three consecutive lines, that possess any metrical exactness—all those melodious passages which have rung upon the ear of Fancy, and shall (in despite of imposture) continue to vibrate there while the nature of man is endowed with poetic feelings, if we believe in this WORM, this *irregular*, *writhing*, and *creeping* inhabitant of the *old* TRUNK, are the innovations of the ignorant, the scorn of the sound critic, and are abjured in the solemn testament

testament of SHAKSPEARE. There is no doubt, that what strikes this writer, will have occurred to the reflection of every judicious reader, namely, the natural and necessary difference between a BOOK, printed hastily from playhouse copies, or peacemeal parts belonging to actors, and the genuine and originating MSS. of the poet. One of the most common press errors arises from the compositor's eye glancing below the following line to that he has composed in what is termed the copy;—hence lines are frequently omitted, hemistichs are wrongly connected; and if we add to this consideration the certainty that common work was never corrected by the author, and that probably a corrector of the press was a character hardly known in a printing office, we have an easy solution of the causes which produced the errors of our early plays. They were printed in haste, and sold probably for less than sixpence. But how arose the palpable errors I have exhibited in the manuscript? Was the meaning clouded in the mind of the greatest genius and most pregnant observer of Nature? Was it his hurry to produce that perplexed his reasoning, defeated its result, perverted his axioms, and mutilated his verse? Was he contented to give to the recitation of skiful actors what no skill could render intelligible to

the

the shrewdest philologist?—Or are we to imagine, that there existed in the manuscript performances of his time certain comprehensive symbols, by which a *word* called up the *idea*, to which it was a clue, and *obscurity* became the beacon to guide them to *clearness?* But the MS. I am reviewing is not the penmanship of idleness. Half the labour bestowed upon unnecessary *letters*, would have cleared away the mystery and and ambiguity of the *meaning*. So much, admitting it for a moment to be genuine—but, whether it be like the MSS. of that time or not, I have I think demonstrated, that its errors are not such as the pen is subject to; but that they are rather those of the press, though certainly more flagrant than those of any press of which we have yet cognizance.

The progress of discussion now leads me to consider those passages of very eminent merit which are not to be found in the book of Mr. Ireland—to determine between us whether, as Mr. Ireland affirms, they are interpolations of the players, or, as this writer confidently maintains they are, authentically Shakspeare's, shall be the task of any man at all conversant with the poet's general manner.

Bastard.

[30]

Bastard. " I promise you the effects he writ of, succeed unhappily, as of unnaturalness betweene the childe and the parent, death, dearth, dissolutions of ancient *armies, divisions in state, menaces and maledictions against king and nobles, needlesse diffidences, banishment of friends, dissipation of cohorts, nuptial breaches, and I know not what.

Edg. " How long have you bin in a sectary astronomical?"
Quarto, 1608.

This passage is not in the folio editions, and for the reasons above given, not in the *MS.* which grounded upon the 2d folio, rarely differs in the progress of the dialogue; but frequently, indeed, by the interspersion of epithets culled out of the quarto.

I have before referred in a note to the 3d scene of the 4th act, which is totally omitted in the folio and the MS. and which could only have been cut out by the players to quicken the action, for, to understand it, the insertion is indispensably necessary, as otherwise the return of the King of France to his own country is left unaccounted for. I have now merely to reprint the passages before quoted and some which follow them—nor shall I apologize for the doing so; they are as worthy of our divine poet as any thing in the play.

* Read *amities.*

Kent.

[31]

Kent. "Did your letters pierce the queen to any demonstra-
"tions of grief?
Gent. "Ay, Sir; she took them, read them in my presence;
"And now and then an ample tear trill'd down
"Her delicate cheek: it seem'd, she was a Queen
"Over her passion; who, most rebel-like,
"Sought to be King o'er her.
Kent. "O, then it mov'd her.
Gent. "Not to a rage: patience and sorrow strove
"Who shou'd express her goodliest. You have seen
"Sunshine and rain at once: her smiles and tears
"Were like a better day: Those happy smiles,
"That play'd on her ripe lip, seem'd not to know
"What guests were in her eyes; which parted thence,
"As pearls from diamonds dropp'd."

After her natural and passionate exclamations upon the inhumanity of her sisters, with a stroke of transcendant pathos, which can be named only, as Theobald has observed, with the action of *Joseph* in sacred writ—

"There she shook
"The holy water from her heavenly eyes,
"And clamour moisten'd: *then away she started*
"*To deal with grief alone.*"

He who can believe that these lines are interpolations by the players falsely deemed beauties, and tending to confuse the detail of the action, is a worthy convert to the Shakspeare MSS. for he has neither taste in sentiment, nor discernment in composition.

The

[32]

The only remaining branch of this enquiry is devoted to a few very bold and hazardous interpolations, which it is humbly conceived by this writer were never seen by Shakspeare, and are yet found in the present publication—from whom they came the reader for himself will " gather " and surmise."

Lear. " Tomm Tomm where dydst steale thyne Adam's Coate"

MARK THE ANSWER.

Edg. " Fromme mye childe anne shedde notte give itte mee
Lear. " A goode Thefte a good Thefte—welle sayde Tomm"

The following splendid addition to the description of Dover Cliff is much too *musical* and apposite to be omitted on the present search after beauties.

Glo. " Butte ist soe have I fallenne or naye
Edg. " Aye formme thys Cliffe thys wònder ò Nature
" Whose chalkye sydes garde thys oure sacredde Isle
" Gaynste the rude Sea that dothé inne cholerre
" Rage foame ande spende itteselfe tylle itte comme toe
" nothynge"

A little on and we are stopt by a couplet, which the writer fancied a pathetic thought, and so no doubt it is, if he knew how to express it.

Leare,

Leare. "Ha Gonerylle whatte flatterre thys white Bearde
"Ande whenne thee pooré dogge dydde fawne and lycke
"thee
"Dydst beate hymme oute a doere Bustle, bustle hygh
"heavenne"

Again,

Leare. "Whenne wee are borne we crye that wee are comme
"To thys sayde stage toe thys sayde *shyppe o fooles*"

Mercy upon his learning! He had procured Barclay's Stultiferum Navis, and no doubt his annotations will be found upon the margin of some rare copy in trunks yet unexplored.

When Lear brings in Cordelia dead in his arms—He most beautifully and tenderly accounts for his hope that she yet lives.

"What is't thou say'st—Her voice was ever soft,
"Gentle and low; an excellent thing in woman."

We are in the MS. infested with a childish amplification, and some lines following so correctly in the style of Pistol, that they provoke laughter.

"Whatte ist thou sayst herre Voyce was everre softe
"Ande lowe *sweete musyck oere the ryplynge streame*
"Qualytye rare ande excellente inne womanne
"*O Yesse bye heavennes twas I kyll'd the slave*
"*Thatte dydde rounde thye softe necke the murderous*
"*Ande damnede Corde entwine*"

F   Instance

Instance the last.

Kente. " Thanks Sir, butte I goe toe thatte unknowne Lande
" Thatte chaynes each Pilgrim faste within its soyle
" Bye livynge menné mouste shunnd mouste dreadèdde
" Stylle mye goode masterre thys same Journey tooke
" Hee calls mee I amme contente ande strayghte obeye
" Thenne farewelle Worlde the busye Sceane is done
" Kente livd mouste true Kente dyes mouste like a manne"

He, who can esteem the above lines, or any of the preceding improvements the production of SHAKSPEARE, may possibly give credit to what is so speedily to follow, I mean

" Here endethe mye Play offe
" Kynge Leare
" Wm Shakspeare"

This examination of Lear is now brought to a close. The man of critical judgment will decide whether the writer has proved the premises stated at the setting out; or whether those of Mr. Ireland in his preface are established by this candid enquiry. If the critic can rely upon principles which he receives as truths—if he can depend upon logic which he has never perverted by sophism, he conceives he has established " that by the gross impurities of the MS. the meaning of many passages is destroyed—that it follows the worst reading where the readings are various —that it cuts the knot of difficulties which a legitimate

gitimate copy would naturally untie—that its interpolations are not in the manner of Shakspeare—and that its orthography bears the character of no period of English literature, except indeed that when the forgeries of CHATTERTON were offered to the public. Of consequence, on the other hand, he concludes, he has refuted the fallacious arguments of the editor in his preface, and demonstrated the book to be without the slightest authority, and one impossible to have ever been the original manuscript of the play in the handwriting of Shakspeare.

With this conviction I now proceed with little apprehension to examine the smaller papers contained in the same volume.

Q. ELIZABETH's LETTER
To SHAKSPEARE.

The Queen with great familiarity is made to compliment " goode Masterre William" upon his prettye verses, and commands him with *his* best actors, to amuse the Court at Hamptowne during the holydayes. Her Majesty graciously adds, " be not slow as the Lord Leicesterre will " bee with usse."

This is addressed to SHAKSPEARE at the Globe, by Thames.—The poet very naturally subscribes this important condescension of the haughtiest of monarchs to a young adventurer, with a request that it may be kept with all possible care.

In the outset of my examination, I confess that having a precept signed by Elizabeth for the Maundy Charities to Maidens now lying before me, I see no very striking difference between that signature and the one to the present letter. If it be forged, it is at least a forgery tolerably skilful.

We have therefore to combat this visual presumption in its favour by an examination of the circumstances stated in the letter. I take the last of these first into consideration—" My Lord " LEICESTER will be with us." I am abundantly satisfied in my own mind, that the latest period in which this nobleman could have attended such " holiday fooleries" was in the summer of 1585, when the great poet was just able to write full man, being born in the year 1564.

My reasons for maintaining this first fact are these. 1. LEICESTER, invested with the high dignity of Lieutenant-General in the Low Countries, landed in *Zeeland* on the 19th December, 1585,

1585.—2. He returned only in the year 1587 for a short space, because his presence in the council was thought essential in the important business of Queen MARY of Scotland—but on the 6th of July of the same year, he again landed in Zeeland, to pursue his vain and imperious challenge of military glory. 3. He was not recalled thence until, says SPEED, her Majesty " knowing that " a kingdom which is divided cannot stand," summoned him to the defence of England, then menaced by the armada of Philip. He commanded at Tilbury in 1588, while the whole nation was in arms, and sunk himself to an inglorious grave, as soon as the menaces of the foe were no longer terrible—for in that year, 1588, Leicester died.

In the year 1585, the great Earl of Southampton became a member of St. John's, Cambridge, resided there 4 years, and when, in 1589, he had taken his Batchelor's degree, he set out upon his travels, being then 16 years of age. We hear much of his gallantry at Paris, and something of his fashionable prodigality—he delighted in play, and, as a nobleman, he played high. It is probable he might return to his native country in the year 1592, when SHAKSPEARE coming to town, and looking about for a patron, dedicates to this illustrious youth his poem of VENUS and ADONIS, entered on the books of the Stationers
Company

Company in the following year, and declared in a most respectful and distant dedication to be the *first heir of his invention.* It no doubt procured him the countenance of this distinguished nobleman, for when he dedicates the TARQUIN and LUCREECE to him in the year 1594, he professes a " love without end," and abates considerably of his formality of address. I am warranted in assuming, that, when he offered Venus and Adonis to SOUTHAMPTON, it was *all* he had to offer, for he " vows to take advantage of all idle hours [those not devoted to his profession as a player] " until he should have honoured him with some " graver labour." Now then I " close with Mr. " IRELAND in the consequence" and demand, in the year 1585, without celebrity as a writer, and certainly having at no period of his life any great merit as an actor, only newly arrived from Stratford, and possessing no patronage, how SHAKSPEARE could attract the royal kindness of ELIZABETH, perform before LEICESTER, and be commanded as the MANAGER of the *Globe Theatre,* not to tarry, but with *his* best players to amuse the sovereign leisure at Hampton? But the GLOBE THEATRE itself was not in existence until eight years after the death of Leicester, viz. 1596[*].

[*] See the works of TAYLOR, the water poet. And a contract between HENSLOWE and PETER STREETE, to build a Playhouse, in the year 1599, exactly similar to that " *new-ly* " *erected* Theatre called the GLOBE, on the Bank."

The

The reader may now surmise why in the MSS. the letter of the Queen has no date—but I have, I trust, relieved him from the dilemma, by shewing, that no date which can be assigned will any way bear out the facts therein asserted.

To the Receipt for FIFTY Pounds by Shakspeare, which follows, for playing before Lord Leicester, from which the date is [*unluckily*] torn off, the same arguments apply with equal force. Lowine, who plays before Leicester also, was then in his 9th year; but, admitting Leicester to have seen plays at his house the year he died, LOWINE could be only 12 years old—he died 1659, aged 83 years.

His Promissory Note to HEMYNGE, which has a date [luckily] 1589, for doing much for him at the GLOBE, and going down to STRATFORD, is also referrable to the same or some of these tests. His friend married in this year, and it is probable was less at leisure than himself to undertake a journey, not, as now, of easy accomplishment.

The Letter to ANNA HATHERREWAYE is [*excuseably*] without date; it is a love-letter.—
The

The internal evidence of sentiment and diction is the only clue to lead us to a just decision. It must, if genuine, have been written at 16 years of age. The expressions " gyldedde bawble " thatte envyronnes the heade of Majestye," " The feelinge thatte didde neareste approache " untoe itte was thatte whiche commethe the " nygheste untoe God meeke ande Gentle Charytye," and " the Cedarre stretchynge forthe " its branches ande succourynge the smallere " Plants from nyppynge winterre orre the boysterouse wyndes," have nothing of the character of our prose in that period of our literature, and are utterly dissimilar from the only specimens of his epistolary style which he has left us. *See the Dedications to* Southampton.

The verses to the same lady are worthy of no other notice, than that they are metrically smooth, a faculty he had lost when he wrote the LEAR *ut supra.*

THE LETTER TO LORD SOUTHAMPTON.

The expressions which challenge the critic here are many. The term *Hys Grace* applied to an earl, I believe, cannot be shewn to be the formulary of the time.—The address *Mye Lorde* is
recent;

recent; and the most indispensable terms "Right Honourable" and " your honour's in all duty," " honourable services," and so on, never once occur, although they constitute nearly all the ceremonial of the age. " *Thryce I have assayed to wryte, and thryce* mye efforts have benne fruitlesse " is a sentence that seems to have been written by a reader of MILTON:

" Thrice he essay'd, and thrice, in spite of scorn,
" Tears, such as angels weep, burst forth."

He is made to say flatly and weakly of gratitude, that it " lulls the *calme* breaste toe softe *softe* repose." To this letter there is no date. His *Grace's* answer has July 4 for the time written, but the year is omitted also, to my great regret. This letter is written in a hand of which I believe the prototype will not easily be found. I have been frustrated in all my researches after the signature of this nobleman. Mr. MALONE is said to possess a legal instrument executed by him, and he will no doubt produce it in his intended examination. To me the internal evidence is sufficient—the following expressions have not the character of the epistolary style of that time.

" As I have been thy friend, so will I continue. Aught that I can do for thee, pray command me, and you fhall find me yours."

The judicious critic at once perceives the modern colouring of diction and flow of language—it is impossible to shew any thing like the above selection in the correspondence of that period.

THE PROFESSION OF FAITH.

My reader will remember, that JOHN SHAKSPEARE, believed to have been the brother of our great poet, composed a paper of this nature, which the industry of the last editors recovered from oblivion.—There was no sufficient reason to be assigned, why the pious disposition of the bard should in so solemn a declaration of opinion be

" Lag of a BROTHER—"

In the volume of Mr. IRELAND there is a profession of faith by WILLIAM SHAKSPEARE, written in the prime and vigour of his life, and in the absolute plenitude of his understanding. He, however, appears so unused to composition of this nature, that he has left us nothing but the peurile quaintness and idiomatic poverty of a Methodist rhapsody.

" I do now in these my serious moments, make this my profession of *faith*, and which I do most solemnly believe." He believes what?
And

[43]

And now methinks I view the reader expecting and preparing for some sublime speculation upon the condition of future existence—and that he who had touched, and with a trembling hand no doubt, the awful ruminations of CLAUDIO, should bequeath to his fellow mortals the rich legacy of his belief and the animating aspiration of his hopes. He believes only what the whole world knows, that " his frail body returns to dust, but for his SOUL—" let GOD judge that as to himself shall seem meet." This is pious acquiescence, but it is not belief. This is followed by some exquisite nonsense, as modern as " this present puny hour " or the writer resigns all pretensions to the power of discrimination.

" Yet will I hope, for even the *poor* Prifoner, when bound with galling Irons, even He will hope for pity, and when the tears of sweet repentance bathe his wretched pillow, he then looks and hopes for pardon."

" O Man, where are thy great, thy boasted attributes, buried, lost *for ever* in *cold* DEATH. O Man, why attemptest thou to search the greatness of the Almighty? thou dost but lose thy labour, more thou attemptest, more thou art lost, till thy poor weak thoughts are elevated to their summit, and then as SNOW from the *leafy* Tree, drop and distill themselves till they are no more."

The above shall pass for piety, if Mr. Ireland pleases, but for SHAKSPEARE's it will never pass

with

with one discerning critic.—The last image needs the specification of an *evergreen* to preserve it from the horticulary censure: of trees, generally speaking, they are denuded of their foliage when the snow falls.

To write with levity upon this subject no good man will be able to do. The following execrable jargon therefore remains without a comment.

"Yet, great God, receive me to thy *bosom*, where all is sweet *content* and *happiness*, all is *bliss*, where *discontent* is never heard, but where one bond of friendship unites all Men. Forgive O Lord, all our sins, and with thy great goodness take us all to thy *breast*—O cherish us like the sweet CHICKEN, that, under the covert of her spreading wings, receives her little brood, and hovering oer them, keeps them harmless and in safety."

As to the letter to COWLEY, with the *Icon* drawn by his own hand, the first ARTISTS of the country tell me, they have no doubt these pen and ink drawings are modern.

DEED OF GIFT TO IRELAND.

"Aye marry! now comes in the sweet of the year."—This is a most delicate bone for the critic cur.

"O, if this had been forgot,
"It had been as a *gap* in our great Feast.
"And all things *gone amiss*."

This

This precious instrument, by which we learn that Shakspeare, " in lieu of the premises " of Masterre WILLIAM HENRY IRELAND's stripping off his *Jerrykyne*, and jumping in Thames after his friend Shakspeare, who was near drowning, in consequence of the " *bayrge-menne* having been merry, doth give to said IRELAND his plays of HENRY IV. and V. King JOHN, and King LEAR—but, what is of more moment than his " *defunct* and *proper* satisfaction " it gives to his Heirs his play, never yet imprinted, named King HENRY THIRD of England—of which more no doubt anon.

Upon the bequests something shall be said, and enough to satisfy any reasonable creature.

The plays of King JOHN, HENRY IV. and V. had been all previously and frequently printed— To what use was a bequest that could never be productive?—How did the said IRELAND ever avail himself of the grateful remuneration? But we have something more to say to him. The play of LEAR is also bequeathed as written at the date of the deed of gift. That date is the 25th day of October 1604.—But LEAR was assuredly not then written: its first appearance on the books of the Stationers' Company is in
Nov.

Nov. 26, 1607, and is there stated to have been played the Christmas preceding before the king—and Mr. MALONE shrewdly determines the period of its first appearance by two circumstances, first, an entry of the old LEAR by way of artifice, on account of the new play, May 8, 1605—and secondly, its alluding to the union of the two kingdoms in name, early in the play.—Now JAMES was proclaimed King of Great Britain October 24, 1604, and with this circumstance in his immediate recollection, the author, in the introduction of an old adage, changed the word Englishman to British-man:

" Fy, fa fum,
" I smell the blood of an Englishman."

See NASH's Pamphlet.

The play was therefore written subsequent to the deed, which, as written, conveys the profits of it to another. The signature here totally departs from the authentic signatures of the poet. To this IRELAND his gratitude seems to have known no bounds of reason or nature.—He says further on

" SHAKSPEARE's *Soule*, restless in the grave
" shall up again and meet his friend his Ireland
" in the blest Court of Heaven.
" O model of Virretue Charitye's sweetest Child
" thy Shakspeare thanks thee. Nor *verse*, nor *sigh*,
" nor *Tear* can say by half how much I love thee."

Such

Such was the *simple* diction of the " spontaneous flow of soul " from our divine poet !! He then, in the language of FALSTAFF, " having much to say of that Ireland," wins five shillings by drawing his house on paper. BASSANIO and SHYLOCK in colours, on paper also, will find critics in every artist.

With respect to the engagements with LOWIN and others at salaries of 1l. 10s. per week—I do not believe that any such engagements were then made in our theatres—but that then, as now in the itinerant companies, the actors played upon *shares* as they are called, and divided according to their value the residue after the managers had been allowed their proportion for house and expences. Besides, the salary is utterly disproportionate to the value of money at the time. Upon the term one pound, I have to remark that Mr. HENSLOW, the proprietor of the Rose Theatre, near the Bank Side, kept his accounts constantly by *shillings* until they came to 3l.—thus,

l.	s.	d.
0.	xxxxiiii.	0
0.	liii.	0 &c. See his papers.

In the lease to the Frazers the Globe is stated to be by the Black Fryers, although if this mean the playhouse of Shakspeare's company, and we
know

[48]

know of no other, it was situated on the Bank Side.

The deed of trust to John Heminge appears a supplement to his Stratford will; however, as the latter revokes all former wills, its dispositions were null and void.—He seems to have conquered, like a good Christian, his aversion to " those of the law " on the 25th March 1616, and to have departed this life the April following in perfect peace with all descriptions of men. His testament is legally made.—The only property Shakspeare recollected then in London was a tenement, wherein one John Robinson dwelt, near the *Wardrobe* in the Black Friars. The only mention of this beloved *Masterre* IRELAND, of whom we hear so much from the new editor, is to be found in the mortgage to HENRY WALKER of that messuage, which is described in the will; it is stated to be then or late in the possession of *one* WILLIAM IRELAND, his assignee or assignees.—He is not by Shakspeare called *William* HENRY, and yet this addition was equally precious; the saver of his life would never by the forgetfulness of Shakspeare have been defrauded of

" Ev'n the slightest worship of his name."

In the curious paper abovementioned, the deed of trust to HEMINGE, he recommends to his care
a certain

a certain boy (indeed an infidel!) who " must not be named," and bequeaths to his *dear Wife* 1801.—so that the Stratford interlineation of the *second best* bed with the furniture had not been so bad a legacy; but, with that instrument revoking all former wills, he contented himself finally with not incurring the imputation of leaving his wife *without a bed to lie on*. They were no doubt alienated from each other's love; he styles her in this last act, *coarsely*, HIS WIFE; and, as he had omitted her in its primitive form, the interlineation expresses the subsequent recollection of her without one epithet of endearment. Can we suppose that his daughters had shut out their mother from his house? Or that if she had been *dear* to him, and needed only a slight token of his love, that this circumstance would have been unmentioned, with some superadded recognition of her dutiful attachment and affectionate care? The mention of her, therefore, in the deed of trust to HEMINGE is a manifest and clumsy intrusion of a *fiction*, resulting from an idle wish to relieve Shakspeare from an imputation, fairly placed, of resenting provocation, the nature and extent of which cannot now be known.

The fragment of HAMLET needs but little of our attention. Its variations from the printed

H   books

books are none of them remarkable, otherways than as they dilute his sense with unmeaning expletives and impede the fluency of his versification. The orthography in the monosyllables is remarkably absurd;—but compared with LEAR, Hamlet is purity. I find, probably a press error, the same *numbers* on two opposite pages, 2 and 3. But the numeration of lines in the drama is I confess a custom to me perfectly recent;—until the present publication, I remember no one example in the collections of old plays. If any work of this nature easily admitted the practice, it was the regular pastoral drama, by FLETCHER, of the *Faithful Shepherdess*—yet that exquisite poem has no such security against intrusion. But if the practice can be supposed to have been then applied to dramatic *metre*, to prose it was absurd to apply it, in a copy meant for the press, where, unless the author correctly knew the number of words contained in the line, the figures would necessarily change their places.

So much for the papers. I have only now to remark upon a few expressions in the preface by their editor. Mr. IRELAND declares that, if he thought it practicable to forge such productions, they should never have appeared. This is an argument from *his* opinion of difficulty—in that

of

of other men, this may be of slighter consequence;—but if we prove them impossible to be genuine, the difficulty is removed by the certainty of its having been surmounted. But the proof of their fallacy in the view of this gentleman places us in a favourable predicament: " We have then *another* SHAKSPEARE!!" To the *possessor* of such treasure, indeed, this can be no dilemma. The muse of Shakspeare, or one equally excellent, will confer the same honour and the same emolument.

But he is persuaded of their authenticity. From his first knowledge of their existence, he has laboured to procure this conviction. Mr. Ireland is not an incurious man—he draws, he engraves, he has a taste for the black letter—his collection is not mean of scarce and valuable literature— he has the patience and the relish of an antiquary. Certainly his opinion is entitled upon this question to more than common consideration.—The difficulty of procuring *paper* of the time, and of imitating the *seals* and *autographs* appears to him insuperable. I am sure I receive this willingly as his real opinion, and observe only how easily we are satisfied upon a discovery which we are interested in believing to be genuine. Yet a moment's reflection, one should think, would be sufficient

sufficient to have convinced a person of such acquirements, that these requisites were certainly attainable. Is it impossible to extract ink from written paper? Or, if this could not be done, are there not blank leaves in the books of public offices, which might without detriment be extracted? I will myself engage to procure him more paper of the time of ELIZABETH in one week, than he can shew me written upon by Shakspeare. If a draughtsman and an engraver do not know how easily the graphic arts can produce such trifles as *seals* and *autographs*, I have only to say—

> "His state is the more gracious;
> "It is a vice to know them."

In the course of the present enquiry, the author may be accused of taking no notice of the conjectural emendations of the MSS. which are in number about 120; the reason shall be given. He cannot receive them, because they in the first place are mere conjectures; and in the second diminish the great mass of impurity, which is a grand argument with him against their reception. One of his strongest positions is, that so foul a transcript could never be the original of the author, and that it must have been utterly unintelligible

[53]

gible if it were. He is made moreover in the deed of gift to Ireland to abjure all amendments, and commands the play to be hereafter printed from this MS. We are therefore to take it exactly as we find it. There are a few errata, I have since perceived in the comments; by which I learn, that Mr. IRELAND had anticipated any ridicule upon the expression " Author of Nature." This work is no otherways an attack upon that gentleman, than as he appears by his criticism to support the publication upon principles which this writer asserts to be fallacious. Controversy can hardly ever be dispassionate. The warmth of the Advocate will be corrected by the calm neutrality of the Judge——that Judge is the PUBLIC.

Nor is the search after truth an object of slight moment in the present instance—if to preserve the integrity of language be useful, and to ascertain the purity of a fountain be important, to those, who must continue in all ages to drink of the stream. It may be said that I have treated the whole with disrespect before I had demonstrated its futility—and this is true.—I was prepared with my whole proof before I began to plead—it is difficult to repress the ardour of conviction.—A General rarely is able to stop the triumph

umph of victory, until he has written a detail of the conflict.

In the contemplation of the PROOF I have here combined, nothing should be despised, because it may be individually *trivial*—when there is an equipoise of evidence a hair will decide the balance. Upon the most minute circumstance overlooked by an impostor, the detection of his fraud may ultimately and solely rest. Neither should that proof be slightingly considered, which depends upon tedious detail and collateral illustration. Upon the first view these papers are amazingly plausible,—DEEDS, LETTERS, POEMS, and PROFESSIONS OF FAITH " *stain'd with the varia-* " *tion of all soils,*" and clothed in a fashion of orthography, which some may think ancient because it is obscure, and genuine because it is unusual. Another and the greatest difficulty to contend against is, that your enemy has, or might have had, the same knowledge of the ground as yourself. But let me be grateful—Circumstances which aided him upon his march, have enabled me to trace his progress. He might have been more circumspect, and rendered detection less easy.—It is, however, probable that eagerness to execute what he had once planned, narrowed his enquiries; and that when he saw the imposing

aspect

[55]

aspect of his design, he overlooked the morbid principle in its *composition*.

This essay is now brought to its conclusion. I trust it has demonstrated that the SMALLER PIECES have not the character of the poet's style, nor the manners of his age—that they are at variance with admitted fact, and disdain good sense not less than they do chronology.

With respect to the Lear, I have opposed the fictitious against the true, and put it in the power of all to decide upon the question. In the doing this, I could not but consider myself in the condition of ARTHEGAL, in the Fairy Queen, who thus opposes the creation of fraud to the pure and genuine FLORIMEL.—I trust and hope the consequence will be the same; and *that*, not so much from motives of personal complacency, as for the credit of English literature.

" Then did he set her by that snowy one,
   " Like the true Saint beside the Image set,
" Of both their beauties to make paragone,
   " And triall whether should the honour get.

" Straightway,

> " Straightway, so soone as both together met,
>   " Th' enchanted damzell vanisht into nought;
>   " Her snowy substance melted as with heat:
> " Ne of that goodly hew remained ought,
> " But th' empty girdle, which about her waste was wrought."
>
> F. Q. b. V. c. iii. s. 24.

I have the honour to be, &c.

JAMES BOADEN.

Warren Street, Fitzroy Square,
11th January, 1796.

EXTRACTS

EXTRACTS FROM VORTIGERN.

THE following appeared in a diurnal publication—Their author has been flattered into a belief, that they merit to be collected. They are therefore attached to this publication, as faint attempts to imitate the inimitable, because, if the play of VORTIGERN, *announced for representation, should, in a trifling degree resemble the great Poet, such partial resemblance may be here shewn not to be decisive of the question of* ORIGINALITY.

SHAKSPEARE.

THE TRAGEDY OF VORTIGERN.

EXTRACT I.

WE have heard much of this play, and the fertility of the ingenious has contrived to elicit no mean amusement from the testimonials in favour of its authenticity: but any thing like a sketch of the FABLE, or an extract from the DIALOGUE, has not yet been offered to the world.

[58]

The following has been transmitted us by a learned friend; and we believe the language will clearly point out the inimitable Author.

Upon the death of CONSTANTINE, King of Britain, while the Nobles hesitated in their choice of a successor, VORTIGERN, Consul of the Gewissens, himself ambitious of the Crown, went to CONSTANS the Monk, and the poet makes him thus address him :—

VORTIGERN.—Constans, this sanctimonious shewe may cheate
The eye that lightly courses o'er the manne,
But thro' the cope's concealing coverture,
The fiery glance of wilde ambition
Flashes its contradiction to the tongue.
O, how mistaken is the credulous manne,
That looks alone for piety inne churchmenne !
There lurks beneath their holy, heavenly seeming,
A fiercer lust of power, than ever flam'd
From mighty combatants.

CONSTANS.—Vaine were denial,
And though secluded by a parent's jealousy,
Deem not I feele the godlike impulse lesse,
Thanne he, who, basking in the sovereign blaze,
Teaches his eye to beare the flame unhurt,
As the young Eagle soaringe to the Sunne.

VORTIGERN.—Your Royal Father's colde and in his shroude;
Your Brothers all incapable of swaye:
Nor see I any member of your race
Whom the sadde people canne preferre to you,

CONSTANS.

Constans.—But thinke upon my Order and my Oathe!
O laye not perjurie upon my soule,
That, vow'd to Heav'n and nothing temporal,
May not encline to your most friendly counsel.

Vortigern.—I'll be your mind's physician, and the people
Leade to demande young Constans for their Sovereigne.

Constans.—My better Father sway me to your pleasure.
And hear me, when the Kingly Chaire is mine
Thy counsel is its basis—every honoure—
Yet what *can* honour thee? shall falle upon thee.

Vortigern.—I'll to my friends; alle needful succoure bringe,
And either die, or consecrate thee Kinge.

[*Exeunt.*]

Vortigern succeeds with the people; and Archbishop Guethelin being dead, and the Clergy refusing to crown a Monk who had abjured his order, Vortigern himself set the crown upon the head of Constans.

But the qualities for government are seldom learned in the Monastery; and Constans, who acquired power, had not sufficient strength of mind to secure it. The designs of Vortigern upon his life, are thus exhibited in a masterly soliloquy, after he has wrought the Picts, whom he left carousing, up to his purposes.

VORTIGERN *solus.*—It cannot faile—I left them flush'd with
    wine;
My well-feign'd wronges, and bounteous largesses,
Have work'd me to their heartes, and not a PICT
But thirsts to plunge a dagger in his bloode.
Yet, should they chill their purpose and reveal me,
Such is my summe of influence and wealthe,
I well might brave avowal. CONSTANS sleeps.
SECURITY seems guardian of his pillow,
But DANGER hides his poinarde in the downe.
What means this tremoure?—O, thou murderous thoughte,
Hast thou more mightye influence than thy acte?
The deed's not done—not doing; yet my flesh
Quivers upon my bones, and this firme trunke
Trembles, as dothe the mountaine oake, before
The lowring threate of the approaching storme.
Hark! hush! what means that wilde and piercing shrieke?
Their rage has rush'd inebriate to his chamber,
And now he dies beneath a thousand armes!
What's best to do? Dissimulation aid me!
I'll to my oratory; for the storme
Will ebbe my waye, and all the wreck's my own.   [*Exit.*]

EXTRACT II.

" THE TRUE CHRONICLE HISTORY OF THE LIFE AND DEATH
OF VORTIGERN, KING OF THE BRITAINES; TOGE-
THER WITH THE LANDING OF HENGIST,
THE SAXON."

Such is the accurate title-page of this exquisite relic of genius. The former analysis brought the
progress

progress of the fable down to the murder of CONSTANS. The next scene shews the murderers bringing in the head of that Monarch to VORTIGERN. He reproaches them bitterly;—sheds a flood of hypocritical tears, and commands their heads to be struck off in London, where the fact was committed.

We are next introduced to the acquaintance of a novel character, a *political* FOOL, to shew the impression of great events upon the domestics of a palace. It has been observed from partial communications, which I have indiscreetly made, that the Fool savours of *Whig doctrines*, and the authenticity of the MSS. has accordingly been impeached; but let any man view the conduct of JAMES I. in the year 1612, when this play was written, and refrain from Whig principles if he can. SHAKSPEARE clearly did not.

SCENE, LONDON—THE PALACE.

Enter the KING'S FOOLE *solus.*

FOOLE.—" I doe much marvelle why Constans woulde be-
" come Kinge at alle—seeing he had neither the valoure whyche
" is nerve, nor the wisdome whyche is experience; nor indeede
" any jot save pietye, which a Christiane Kinge oughte to have.
" He was not maistere of his crafte, else hadde this Vortigerne's
" hedde beene now silente, who gives the cue o'the courtiers,
" and commaunds the ducks o'the rabble.

" I shalle

" I shalle never forgette the sighte o'his pill'd crowne, whenne
" the Pictishmenne set upon him. Had his haires been lives
" he had beene satisfied; yet I wronge them, for you may
" sweare he hadde a poore groats-worthe of haire, seeinge he
" was polled so rawlye. His last croppe is a legasey to his
" Convente, and we shall see miracles worked with it anon.

" Welle, nowe is this Vortigerne Kinge, beshrewe the chance,
" for a Foole wille never be the better for him! Mercy upon
" the people, they are never soe safe as whenne a Monarche
" weares motley.—You shalle have some wille cry out on va-
" loure and wisdome, to begette foreigne expedition and home
" pillage; but commende mee to the gilt codpiece and a cappe
" with belles."

Enter GEOFRID.

GEO.—" How nowe foole, what wrapped in humourous
" contemplation. Art thou sadde at the newe succession to the
" olde throne?"

FOOLE.—" Youre pardonne, Sir; marvelous gladde, I as-
" sure you."

GEO.—" Why gladde, foole?"

FOOLE.—" That wee have a chance of amendmente."

GEO.—" See you not rather a chance of becoming worse?"

FOOLE.—" Heaven helpe your hedde! marke the wordes of
" the foole. The newe Lordes o'the Courte wille stand upon
" their courtesey, to shew they merit their places; and the
" olde are sette upon their mettle, lest the new comers should
" pushe them from their chaires. Marrye if you would have
" a manne do his dutye, shewe that others are readye to per-
" forme it, if he faile."

GEOFRID

Geofrid then enters into a panegyric upon the character of Constans, or to latinize it farther, Constantius, and describes the manner of his death; his kneeling, and with open arms receiving the swords of the assassins.

> " With outstretch'd armes he welcomed ruines breache,
> " By which a floode of glorye entered,
> " And smilinglye his bodye sunke to peace."

The next extract will shew the arrival of Hengist, and the address of that Saxon adventurer, the attraction of Vortigern by the daughter Rowena, and the stratagems by which her father grew important to the state.

Extract III.

The last number of these Extracts left Vortigern in the possession of the crown of Constantius, whom he had caused to be murdered. We are now to notice the flight of the late King's brothers, Aurelius Ambrosius, and Uther Pendragon. They seek a refuge in Lesser Britain, and levy troops against the murtherous usurper.

Things are in this state, Vortigern at Canterbury, in a favourite palace, when he is informed
of

of the arrival of a band of TALL STRANGERS, in large ships, who demand admittance to his presence. They are courteously introduced in the following scene—

COURTE AT CANTORBERIE.

TRUMPETTES SOUNDE A SENETTE.

Entere, in his Robes of Audience, VORTIGERNE *and his Nobles. One introduceth* HENGIST, HORSUS, *and the reste of their meynie—with the* FOOLE.

HENG.—Most Noble Kinge, from Germany wee come,
And Saxonie the province of oure birthe.
Th' occasione is to tender our assistance
Even unto you, or to some othere Prince.
Custome, whose sovereigne and imperious rule
Nô earthlye breathe may ere withstande, decrees
That wee shoulde seeke a foreign soile and service,
Our Country's superfluitie caste forthe.
Nor deeme ye lightlye of the proffer'd ayde;
The bloode of Goddes doth flowe withinne these veines,
Grandsonnes of WODEN, underre whose safe guidance
Our sturdie keeles are grounded on youre shores.

VORT.—Warrioures, I neede not spende the time with vaine
And emptie salutatione, courtesie
Shoulde stille be founde in Courtes, or they muste change
Theire nature, and that gentle powere ittes name.
Of WODEN I have hearde, the heathene worlde
Terme him slye MERCURIE, the winged Godde,
Who makes the aire his Pegassus, and rides
Upon the bleake and barren gales that blowe
From the farre corners of the frozenne Northe.

FOOLE

FOOLE (*Aside.*)—Yes, a manne woulde sweare they came here undere the conduct of Mercury, they are so sure *conveyancers*. Whenne they sette foote at Dover, they scrambled mee uppe the Cliffes after the muttons, as the goate upon the cragges, where the sweete mosse growes. You had a sumptious banket upon the summite before you coulde take offe a castore—butte marry no marvelle, theire patrone stole them fire fromme Heavene, and not to wante savorie sawce, they whipt mee up the samphire menne as they ascended, bagge and stowage, as they hunge dangling from theire poles like soe manye whirlebattes.

HENG.—For our religione, Kinge, knowe thatte wee worshippe
WODEN especially, who gives name
To the fourthe daye of everye weeke of time.
Nexte to himme wee adore the Goddesse FREA,
Fromme whome the sixthe daye claimes ittes honoured name.

FOOLE.—Kinsmenne, I salute youe alle. Our affinitie is closere than bloode canne make itte. We have the same parents, Necessitie, the mothere of all inventive expeditiones. Whatte renders you talle adventurers, makes mee jestere to the Courte.

HENG.—Goode Foole, lette mee have youre goode reporte.

FOOLE.—Godde forbide; I canne do you no goode—Youe do notte come, as I take itte, on a businesse of *jeste*; and I doe most potentlie believe yee will be founde to be in earneste. Marke the prophecie of MERLIN, Kinge, and perpende.

VORT.—I have considered of youre bounteous proffere,
And taken counsaile of our pressinge neede;
Againste oure enemie wee shall employe ye,
Nowe from Albania issuinge on the land:
And thoughe youre faithlesse worshippe I lamente,
Wee doe accepte youre love with high contente.

[*Exeunt*].

K   FOOLE.

Foole.—Here's a holye compacte! This Vortigerne makes noe more of a mannes life thanne to counte five, and yette he lamentes a knaves pietie to his grandfathere. Whye was I borne a foole, and thus compelled to smelle oute the knaverie of the worlde! Happie is the casuist! he canne solve alle scruples, and reconcile the only shrewde foes o' the peace, conscience, and intereste.

Extract IV.

The last of these popular extracts brought the fable down to the king's acceptance of the services of Hengist, with which the first act closes. The second act opens with Hengist entertaining Vortigern at a banquet, and when the guests were filled with wine he introduced his daughter Rowena, the most beautiful woman of Germany.

She salutes Vortigern in her own tongue, with the words so long remembered—

Entere Rowena, *sumtuously attired,*
Bearing a golden Chalice.

Row.—Laverd Kinge, wacht heil.
[*She courteouslye bendeth.*]

Vort.—What paragone of earthlye excellence,
Or rather saye, what heavenlye habitante,
Hathe lefte her sphere of blessednesse and joye
To putte to shame the brightest of oure beauties?

Whatte

Whatte sayes she, WOORDEN, bye mye hallidome,
Her salutatione claimes a faire replye.

   WOOR.—Her wordes are these, " LORD KINGE, I drinke
      youre healthe,
Youre Majestie, in pledge, must saye, *drinc heil.*

   VORT.—Drinc heil, then saye I, by your leave,
      sweete Princesse,
Thus on youre lippes wee tender you oure love.

———

The next scene discovers VORTIGERN, with his favourite Minister in the Royal Cabinet; to whom he relates the last adventure, and expresses his determination to demand ROWENA of her father. The MINISTER, like an honest man, remonstrates thus:

   MIN.—I hadde not hearde your Majestie soe farre,
But thatte a most usurpinge wonder stole
Discernmente from youre lowly servantes minde.
Whatte counsaile maye availe, (yet whatte can counsaile
Againste imperial love?) shalle be assayde.
O thinke, deare Liege, upon youre presente Queene!
Thinke inne whatte true allegiance shee has lived
For twentie yeares youre wife; and in thatte time
Hathe bless'd this realme with many princely pledges:
The floure of Britains—Bye the sainted chaire
Of holie Paule, a Ladye yette mòre faire,
More meeklye pious and more lowlie wise,
Breathes not the aire of hallowed Christendome.

———

It may readily be imagined, that talking thus of stale charms and cloistered merits to a king blinded by *passion*, and eager for *enjoyment*, would have but slender influence. Vortigern replies only by a rapturous description of that beauty which had so inflamed him.

Vort.—I telle thee Seofrid her approache didde seeme
Like the proude swanne's, that glides adowne the streame,
When wondringe croudes do gaze upon her beautie.
She, in her hearte elate, dothe arche her necke,
And bendinge viewes her whitenesse in the wave.

Min.—Rowena, gracious Sovereigne, is a pagane;
Admitted bee her charmmes it skilles not here.

Vort.—[*Not attendinge to his counsaile.*]
Her breastes were two faire hilles, upon whose toppes
The dazzlinge chastitie of snowe didde reste:
Whyle from her eyes a holie fire didde streame,
Thatte, whyle it kindled flame in grosser moulde,
Lefte those pure icye summits ever colde.
Yette on her cheekes such flushing brightness spreade,
As the softe cloudes beares whenne the amorous sunne
Caressesse them, and blushes painte the Weste.

☞ Our next Extract will introduce a new personage, Vortimer, the excellent son of an unworthy king.

Extract

Extract V.

The last number of the extracts presented a very highly-finished portrait of Rowena, and exhibited the King in a state greatly prejudicial to the rights of his Queen and the hopes of his son. We now go to shew the influence of this passion at Court.

THE COURTE.

SCENE—AN INNERE CHAMBER.

Enter the Foole *melancholique.*

Thoughe I am but as you woulde saye a foole, yette I can see how this worlde wagges. Alle is but motley. Youre silken Sovereigne and youre worsted-stocken knave are but variable services, two conditions but to one ende. Nowe is the Courte clefte in twaine like the crowne of an egge, and the meate o' the Monarchie is a preye to youre adventurer. The olde Queene is in extremitie, ande neare her ende ; the yonge one has the grace of noveltie to recommende her to mye grace; but shee neither understands mye witte nor I hers. Yette can a manne offer to sweare which hath the better ende of the staffe. How shalle the foole choose ? lookye, here stands olde virtue in cyprus lawne—by mye faye, a goodlye marble for a cloystere niche! There stands youthfulle beauty in buffe and brooches, owches and carkanetttes. What sayes the poore fleshe on one hande; howe saye youe, conscience, on the othere? Whye, as none but a foole woulde preferre mortification to
pleasure'

pleasure, soe the olde Courte shalle be the choyce of the foole.
Mye olde mistresse wille at leaste be worthe a jeste undere alle
her sorrowes.   [*Exit.*

Enter VORTIMER, *the* Kinges sonne.

Howe alle these changes come full-sumd together
Like flocks of fowle migrating to the Southe,
Evn in their passage met by bolder winges,
Whiche finde theire winter temperate and kinde.
Thus Hengist seekes the storme wee shudder atte,
Ande buildes his castle onne oure faithlesse sande.
Howe stande mye rights then in the greate accounte?
A father snared—a virtuous mothere shamd—
And foreign beautye climbinge to the throne
Like VENUS shielded by the maile of MARRS!
The BRITONS soured bye discontente, are fledde,
And none but Saxons now adorne the Courte,
Or rather saye they guarde thanne grace the Kinge.
Mye father lookes but with Rowena's eyes,
And they with murky frowns doe loure upon mee,
Threateninge like heavy cloudes in summers haunche
The nimble hatred of the lighteninges hidden!
Whatte if I flye and hedde the Britaine bandes!
Howe Vortimer! a rebell to thy Kinge!
Thatte Kinge a father too! O wretched state!—
O bosome, tortured betweene love and dutye!—
Maye notte hostilitye at times be mercye,
As the wise Leeche from bodilye gangreene
Preserves the noble partes by amputatioun?
Hence to ARMORICA! this truthe Ile shewe,
A filial dutye in a seeminge foe!
Lette Heaven but shape mye endes!

———

The

The next passage forcibly reminds the reader of As You Like It.—The scene discovers Vortigern's Queen, attended by the faithful Fool, journeying through a wood—he attempts to chear her under the pressure of her misfortunes.

SCENE—A WOODE.

Storme hearde.

Enter VORTIGERNES QUEENE *and the* FOOLE.

QUEENE.—The storme growes lowder, and the angrye heavens
Doe write theire wrathe in characters of fire,
The blinde might reade and tremble.

FOOLE.—Nay, he might tremble for that mattere before he reade. Truly the lessone is sulpherous enough, you maye smelle out its meaninge. Are you notte afearde Ladye?

QUEENE.—Feare is for VORTIGERNE. The guiltye tremble.
And, whenne the forked lightninge splits the OAKE,
Shrinke at the warninge of the thunderes voice.
The virtuous, like the tender MYRTLE, bende
Beneathe the blaste—no enemye to them.

FOOLE.—The Foole I see thenne hath a knavish coveringe. [*It thundereth againe.*] There againe Madame. I had rathere he mye Ladye o'the broache, and runne by the fireside of a Courte kitchen, than contende with this strange fire that roastes a manne alive.

QUEENE.—Go thenne, poor KNAVE, consult thye bodies
   comforte.
Gette thee to Courte againe, feede and be merye.
Thy Mistresse, Boy, canne wander forthe alone;
Alle daye can journeye onne the flintye roade,
And, whenne the nighte comes, and the sleepless windes
Doe walke on their greate errandes, lay mee downe
On some wilde bedde, composed of withered leaves,
Thenne praise our Goddes, and feare no fairye tempter.

F I N I S.